My Personal Details

Name ————————————————————

Adress ————————————————————

Insurance Company ————————————

Phone ————————————————————

Car Details

Year ————————————————————

Make ————————————————————

Model ————————————————————

Engine Oil Type ————————————————

Purchase date ——————————————

Price ————————————————————

Mileage at Purchase ————————————

Purchased From ——————————————

Date	Mileage	Oil Changed	Rotate/Balance Tires	Air Filters	Tires Replaced	Battery Replaced	Brakes Serviced	Belts & hoses Checked	Wheel alignment	Radiator	Viper Blades	Transmission	Car washed	Cost

Other Maintenance		
Date/ Time	Destination/ Place	Mileage

Date	Mileage	Oil Changed	Rotate/Balance Tires	Air Filters	Tires Replaced	Battery Replaced	Brakes Serviced	Belts & hoses Checked	Wheel alignment	Radiator	Viper Blades	Transmission	Car washed	Cost

Other Maintenance		
Date/ Time	Destination/ Place	Mileage

Date	Mileage	Oil Changed	Rotate/Balance Tires	Air Filters	Tires Replaced	Battery Replaced	Brakes Serviced	Belts & hoses Checked	Wheel alignment	Radiator	Viper Blades	Transmission	Car washed	Cost

Other Maintenance		
Date/ Time	Destination/ Place	Mileage

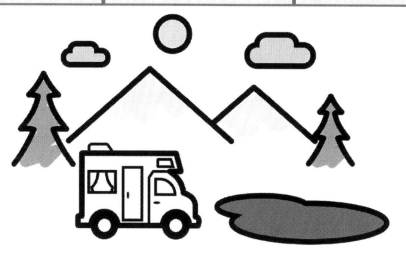

Date	Mileage	Oil Changed	Rotate/Balance Tires	Air Filters	Tires Replaced	Battery Replaced	Brakes Serviced	Belts & hoses Checked	Wheel alignment	Radiator	Viper Blades	Transmission	Car washed	Cost

Other Maintenance		
Date/ Time	Destination/ Place	Mileage

Date	Mileage	Oil Changed	Rotate/Balance Tires	Air Filters	Tires Replaced	Battery Replaced	Brakes Serviced	Belts & hoses Checked	Wheel alignment	Radiator	Viper Blades	Transmission	Car washed	Cost

Other Maintenance		
Date/ Time	Destination/ Place	Mileage

Date	Mileage	Oil Changed	Rotate/ Balance Tires	Air Filters	Tires Replaced	Battery Replaced	Brakes Serviced	Belts & hoses Checked	Wheel alignment	Radiator	Viper Blades	Transmission	Car washed	Cost

Other Maintenance		
Date/ Time	Destination/ Place	Mileage

Date	Mileage	Oil Changed	Rotate/Balance Tires	Air Filters	Tires Replaced	Battery Replaced	Brakes Serviced	Belts & hoses Checked	Wheel alignment	Radiator	Viper Blades	Transmission	Car washed	Cost

Other Maintenance		
Date/ Time	Destination/ Place	Mileage

Date	Mileage	Oil Changed	Rotate/Balance Tires	Air Filters	Tires Replaced	Battery Replaced	Brakes Serviced	Belts & hoses Checked	Wheel alignment	Radiator	Viper Blades	Transmission	Car washed	Cost

Other Maintenance		
Date/ Time	Destination/ Place	Mileage

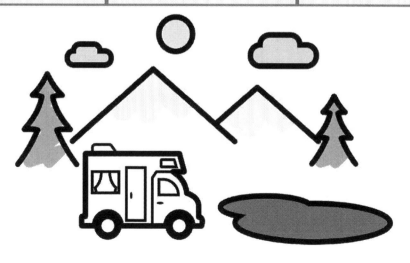

Date	Mileage	Oil Changed	Rotate/Balance Tires	Air Filters	Tires Replaced	Battery Replaced	Brakes Serviced	Belts & hoses Checked	Wheel alignment	Radiator	Viper Blades	Transmission	Car washed	Cost

Other Maintenance		
Date/ Time	Destination/ Place	Mileage

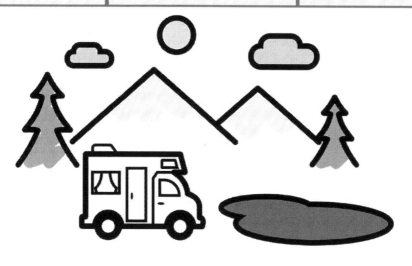

Date	Mileage	Oil Changed	Rotate/Balance Tires	Air Filters	Tires Replaced	Battery Replaced	Brakes Serviced	Belts & hoses Checked	Wheel alignment	Radiator	Viper Blades	Transmission	Car washed	Cost

Other Maintenance		
Date/ Time	Destination/ Place	Mileage

Date	Mileage	Oil Changed	Rotate/Balance Tires	Air Filters	Tires Replaced	Battery Replaced	Brakes Serviced	Belts & hoses Checked	Wheel alignment	Radiator	Viper Blades	Transmission	Car washed	Cost

Other Maintenance		
Date/ Time	Destination/ Place	Mileage

Date	Mileage	Oil Changed	Rotate/Balance Tires	Air Filters	Tires Replaced	Battery Replaced	Brakes Serviced	Belts & hoses Checked	Wheel alignment	Radiator	Viper Blades	Transmission	Car washed	Cost

Other Maintenance		
Date/ Time	Destination/ Place	Mileage

Date	Mileage	Oil Changed	Rotate/ Balance Tires	Air Filters	Tires Replaced	Battery Replaced	Brakes Serviced	Belts & hoses Checked	Wheel alignment	Radiator	Viper Blades	Transmission	Car washed	Cost

Other Maintenance		
Date/ Time	Destination/ Place	Mileage

Date	Mileage	Oil Changed	Rotate/Balance Tires	Air Filters	Tires Replaced	Battery Replaced	Brakes Serviced	Belts & hoses Checked	Wheel alignment	Radiator	Viper Blades	Transmission	Car washed	Cost

Other Maintenance		
Date/ Time	Destination/ Place	Mileage

Date	Mileage	Oil Changed	Rotate/Balance Tires	Air Filters	Tires Replaced	Battery Replaced	Brakes Serviced	Belts & hoses Checked	Wheel alignment	Radiator	Viper Blades	Transmission	Car washed	Cost

Other Maintenance		
Date/ Time	Destination/ Place	Mileage

Date	Mileage	Oil Changed	Rotate/Balance Tires	Air Filters	Tires Replaced	Battery Replaced	Brakes Serviced	Belts & hoses Checked	Wheel alignment	Radiator	Viper Blades	Transmission	Car washed	Cost

Other Maintenance		
Date/ Time	Destination/ Place	Mileage

Date	Mileage	Oil Changed	Rotate/Balance Tires	Air Filters	Tires Replaced	Battery Replaced	Brakes Serviced	Belts & hoses Checked	Wheel alignment	Radiator	Viper Blades	Transmission	Car washed	Cost

Other Maintenance		
Date/ Time	Destination/ Place	Mileage

Date	Mileage	Oil Changed	Rotate/ Balance Tires	Air Filters	Tires Replaced	Battery Replaced	Brakes Serviced	Belts & hoses Checked	Wheel alignment	Radiator	Viper Blades	Transmission	Car washed	Cost

Other Maintenance		
Date/ Time	Destination/ Place	Mileage

Date	Mileage	Oil Changed	Rotate/Balance Tires	Air Filters	Tires Replaced	Battery Replaced	Brakes Serviced	Belts & hoses Checked	Wheel alignment	Radiator	Viper Blades	Transmission	Car washed	Cost

Other Maintenance		
Date/ Time	Destination/ Place	Mileage

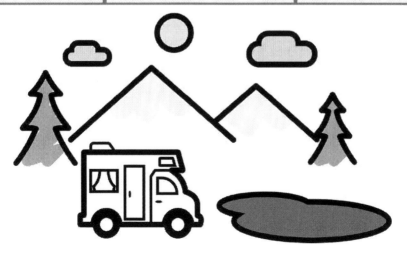

Date	Mileage	Oil Changed	Rotate/ Balance Tires	Air Filters	Tires Replaced	Battery Replaced	Brakes Serviced	Belts & hoses Checked	Wheel alignment	Radiator	Viper Blades	Transmission	Car washed	Cost

Other Maintenance

Date/ Time	Destination/ Place	Mileage

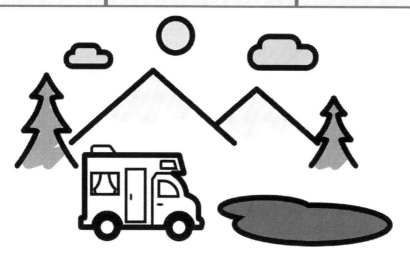

Date	Mileage	Oil Changed	Rotate/Balance Tires	Air Filters	Tires Replaced	Battery Replaced	Brakes Serviced	Belts & hoses Checked	Wheel alignment	Radiator	Viper Blades	Transmission	Car washed	Cost

Other Maintenance		
Date/ Time	Destination/ Place	Mileage

Date	Mileage	Oil Changed	Rotate/Balance Tires	Air Filters	Tires Replaced	Battery Replaced	Brakes Serviced	Belts & hoses Checked	Wheel alignment	Radiator	Viper Blades	Transmission	Car washed	Cost

Other Maintenance		
Date/ Time	Destination/ Place	Mileage

Date	Mileage	Oil Changed	Rotate/Balance Tires	Air Filters	Tires Replaced	Battery Replaced	Brakes Serviced	Belts & hoses Checked	Wheel alignment	Radiator	Viper Blades	Transmission	Car washed	Cost

Other Maintenance		
Date/ Time	Destination/ Place	Mileage

Date	Mileage	Oil Changed	Rotate/ Balance Tires	Air Filters	Tires Replaced	Battery Replaced	Brakes Serviced	Belts & hoses Checked	Wheel alignment	Radiator	Viper Blades	Transmission	Car washed	Cost

Other Maintenance

Date/ Time	Destination/ Place	Mileage

Date	Mileage	Oil Changed	Rotate / Balance Tires	Air Filters	Tires Replaced	Battery Replaced	Brakes Serviced	Belts & hoses Checked	Wheel alignment	Radiator	Viper Blades	Transmission	Car washed	Cost

Other Maintenance		
Date/ Time	Destination/ Place	Mileage

Date	Mileage	Oil Changed	Rotate/Balance Tires	Air Filters	Tires Replaced	Battery Replaced	Brakes Serviced	Belts & hoses Checked	Wheel alignment	Radiator	Viper Blades	Transmission	Car washed	Cost

Other Maintenance		
Date/ Time	Destination/ Place	Mileage

Date	Mileage	Oil Changed	Rotate/ Balance Tires	Air Filters	Tires Replaced	Battery Replaced	Brakes Serviced	Belts & hoses Checked	Wheel alignment	Radiator	Viper Blades	Transmission	Car washed	Cost

Other Maintenance		
Date/ Time	Destination/ Place	Mileage

Date	Mileage	Oil Changed	Rotate/Balance Tires	Air Filters	Tires Replaced	Battery Replaced	Brakes Serviced	Belts & hoses Checked	Wheel alignment	Radiator	Viper Blades	Transmission	Car washed	Cost

Other Maintenance		
Date/ Time	Destination/ Place	Mileage

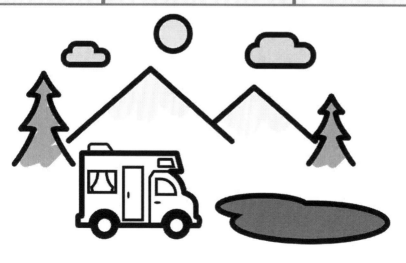

Date	Mileage	Oil Changed	Rotate/ Balance Tires	Air Filters	Tires Replaced	Battery Replaced	Brakes Serviced	Belts & hoses Checked	Wheel alignment	Radiator	Viper Blades	Transmission	Car washed	Cost

Other Maintenance		
Date/ Time	Destination/ Place	Mileage

Date	Mileage	Oil Changed	Rotate/Balance Tires	Air Filters	Tires Replaced	Battery Replaced	Brakes Serviced	Belts & hoses Checked	Wheel alignment	Radiator	Viper Blades	Transmission	Car washed	Cost

Other Maintenance		
Date/ Time	Destination/ Place	Mileage

Date	Mileage	Oil Changed	Rotate/Balance Tires	Air Filters	Tires Replaced	Battery Replaced	Brakes Serviced	Belts & hoses Checked	Wheel alignment	Radiator	Viper Blades	Transmission	Car washed	Cost

Other Maintenance		
Date/ Time	Destination/ Place	Mileage

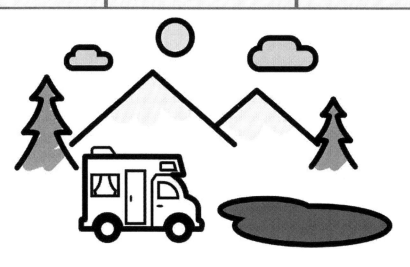

Date	Mileage	Oil Changed	Rotate/Balance Tires	Air Filters	Tires Replaced	Battery Replaced	Brakes Serviced	Belts & hoses Checked	Wheel alignment	Radiator	Viper Blades	Transmission	Car washed	Cost

Other Maintenance		
Date/ Time	Destination/ Place	Mileage

Date	Mileage	Oil Changed	Rotate/ Balance Tires	Air Filters	Tires Replaced	Battery Replaced	Brakes Serviced	Belts & hoses checked	Wheel alignment	Radiator	Viper Blades	Transmission	Car washed	Cost

Other Maintenance		
Date/ Time	Destination/ Place	Mileage

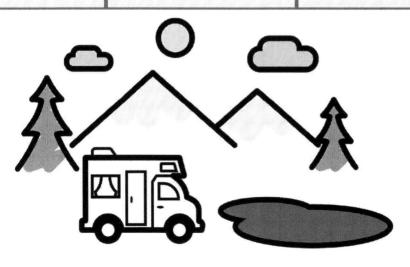

Date	Mileage	Oil Changed	Rotate/ Balance Tires	Air Filters	Tires Replaced	Battery Replaced	Brakes Serviced	Belts & hoses Checked	Wheel alignment	Radiator	Viper Blades	Transmission	Car washed	Cost

Other Maintenance		
Date/ Time	Destination/ Place	Mileage

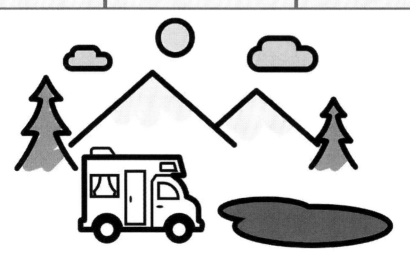

Date	Mileage	Oil Changed	Rotate/ Balance Tires	Air Filters	Tires Replaced	Battery Replaced	Brakes Serviced	Belts & hoses checked	Wheel alignment	Radiator	Viper Blades	Transmission	Car washed	Cost

Other Maintenance		
Date/ Time	Destination/ Place	Mileage

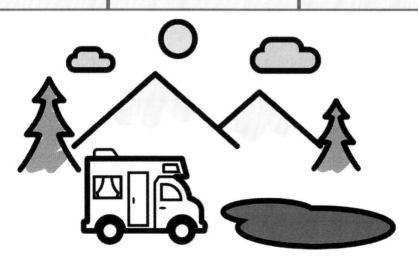

Date	Mileage	Oil Changed	Rotate/ Balance Tires	Air Filters	Tires Replaced	Battery Replaced	Brakes Serviced	Belts & hoses Checked	Wheel alignment	Radiator	Viper Blades	Transmission	Car washed	Cost

Other Maintenance		
Date/ Time	Destination/ Place	Mileage

Date	Mileage	Oil Changed	Rotate/Balance Tires	Air Filters	Tires Replaced	Battery Replaced	Brakes Serviced	Belts & hoses checked	Wheel alignment	Radiator	Viper Blades	Transmission	Car washed	Cost

Other Maintenance		
Date/ Time	Destination/ Place	Mileage

Date	Mileage	Oil Changed	Rotate/ Balance Tires	Air Filters	Tires Replaced	Battery Replaced	Brakes Serviced	Belts & hoses Checked	Wheel alignment	Radiator	Viper Blades	Transmission	Car washed	Cost

Other Maintenance		
Date/ Time	Destination/ Place	Mileage

Date	Mileage	Oil Changed	Rotate/ balance Tires	Air Filters	Tires Replaced	Battery Replaced	Brakes Serviced	Belts & hoses checked	Wheel alignment	Radiator	Viper Blades	Transmission	Car washed	Cost

Other Maintenance		
Date/ Time	Destination/ Place	Mileage

Date	Mileage	Oil Changed	Rotate/Balance Tires	Air Filters	Tires Replaced	Battery Replaced	Brakes Serviced	Belts & hoses Checked	Wheel alignment	Radiator	Viper Blades	Transmission	Car washed	Cost

Other Maintenance		
Date/ Time	Destination/ Place	Mileage

Date	Mileage	Oil Changed	Rotate/ Balance Tires	Air Filters	Tires Replaced	Battery Replaced	Brakes Serviced	Belts & hoses Checked	Wheel alignment	Radiator	Viper Blades	Transmission	Car washed	Cost

Other Maintenance		
Date/ Time	Destination/ Place	Mileage

Date	Mileage	Oil Changed	Rotate/ Balance Tires	Air Filters	Tires Replaced	Battery Replaced	Brakes Serviced	Belts & hoses Checked	Wheel alignment	Radiator	Viper Blades	Transmission	Car washed	Cost

Other Maintenance		
Date/ Time	Destination/ Place	Mileage

Date	Mileage	Oil Changed	Rotate/ Balance Tires	Air Filters	Tires Replaced	Battery Replaced	Brakes Serviced	Belts & hoses Checked	Wheel alignment	Radiator	Viper Blades	Transmission	Car washed	Cost

Other Maintenance		
Date/ Time	Destination/ Place	Mileage

Date	Mileage	Oil Changed	Rotate / Balance Tires	Air Filters	Tires Replaced	Battery Replaced	Brakes Serviced	Belts & hoses Checked	Wheel alignment	Radiator	Viper Blades	Transmission	Car washed	Cost

Other Maintenance		
Date/ Time	Destination/ Place	Mileage

Date	Mileage	Oil Changed	Rotate/ Balance Tires	Air Filters	Tires Replaced	Battery Replaced	Brakes Serviced	Belts & hoses Checked	Wheel alignment	Radiator	Viper Blades	Transmission	Car washed	Cost

Other Maintenance		
Date/ Time	Destination/ Place	Mileage

Date	Mileage	Oil Changed	Rotate/ Balance Tires	Air Filters	Tires Replaced	Battery Replaced	Brakes Serviced	Belts & hoses Checked	Wheel alignment	Radiator	Viper Blades	Transmission	Car washed	Cost

Other Maintenance

Date/ Time	Destination/ Place	Mileage

Date	Mileage	Oil Changed	Rotate/ Balance Tires	Air Filters	Tires Replaced	Battery Replaced	Brakes Serviced	Belts & hoses checked	Wheel alignment	Radiator	Viper Blades	Transmission	Car washed	Cost

Other Maintenance		
Date/ Time	Destination/ Place	Mileage

Date	Mileage	Oil Changed	Rotate/ Balance Tires	Air Filters	Tires Replaced	Battery Replaced	Brakes Serviced	Belts & hoses Checked	Wheel alignment	Radiator	Viper Blades	Transmission	Car washed	Cost

Other Maintenance		
Date/ Time	Destination/ Place	Mileage

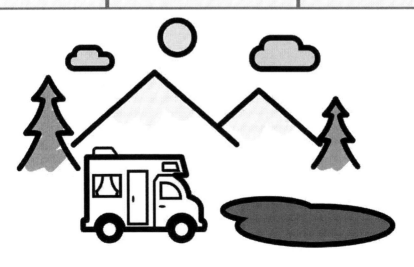

Date	Mileage	Oil Changed	Rotate/ Balance Tires	Air Filters	Tires Replaced	Battery Replaced	Brakes Serviced	Belts & hoses checked	Wheel alignment	Radiator	Viper Blades	Transmission	Car washed	Cost

Other Maintenance		
Date/ Time	Destination/ Place	Mileage

Date	Mileage	Oil Changed	Rotate/balance Tires	Air Filters	Tires Replaced	Battery Replaced	Brakes Serviced	Belts & hoses Checked	Wheel alignment	Radiator	Viper Blades	Transmission	Car washed	Cost

Other Maintenance		
Date/ Time	Destination/ Place	Mileage

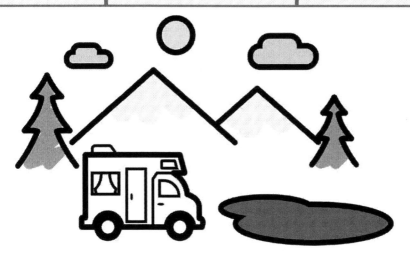

Date	Mileage	Oil Changed	Rotate/ balance Tires	Air Filters	Tires Replaced	Battery Replaced	Brakes Serviced	Belts & hoses checked	Wheel alignment	Radiator	Viper Blades	Transmission	Car washed	Cost

Other Maintenance		
Date/ Time	Destination/ Place	Mileage

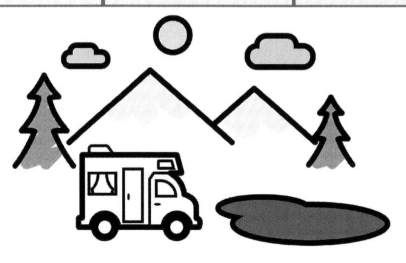

Date	Mileage	Oil Changed	Rotate/ Balance Tires	Air Filters	Tires Replaced	Battery Replaced	Brakes Serviced	Belts & hoses checked	Wheel alignment	Radiator	Viper Blades	Transmission	Car washed	Cost

Other Maintenance		
Date/ Time	Destination/ Place	Mileage

Date	Mileage	Oil Changed	Rotate/ Balance Tires	Air Filters	Tires Replaced	Battery Replaced	Brakes Serviced	Belts & hoses checked	Wheel alignment	Radiator	Viper Blades	Transmission	Car washed	Cost

Other Maintenance

Date/ Time	Destination/ Place	Mileage

Date	Mileage	Oil Changed	Rotate/ Balance Tires	Air Filters	Tires Replaced	Battery Replaced	Brakes Serviced	Belts & hoses Checked	Wheel alignment	Radiator	Viper Blades	Transmission	Car washed	Cost

Other Maintenance		
Date/ Time	Destination/ Place	Mileage

Date	Mileage	Oil Changed	Rotate/ Balance Tires	Air Filters	Tires Replaced	Battery Replaced	Brakes Serviced	Belts & hoses Checked	Wheel alignment	Radiator	Viper Blades	Transmission	Car washed	Cost

Other Maintenance		
Date/ Time	Destination/ Place	Mileage

Date	Mileage	Oil Changed	Rotate/Balance Tires	Air Filters	Tires Replaced	Battery Replaced	Brakes Serviced	Belts & hoses Checked	Wheel alignment	Radiator	Viper Blades	Transmission	Car washed	Cost

Other Maintenance		
Date/ Time	Destination/ Place	Mileage

Date	Mileage	Oil Changed	Rotate/ Balance Tires	Air Filters	Tires Replaced	Battery Replaced	Brakes Serviced	Belts & hoses Checked	Wheel alignment	Radiator	Viper Blades	Transmission	Car washed	Cost

Other Maintenance		
Date/ Time	Destination/ Place	Mileage

Date	Mileage	Oil Changed	Rotate/ balance Tires	Air Filters	Tires Replaced	Battery Replaced	Brakes Serviced	Belts & hoses checked	Wheel alignment	Radiator	Viper Blades	Transmission	Car washed	Cost

Other Maintenance		
Date/ Time	Destination/ Place	Mileage

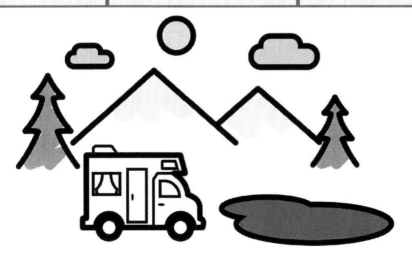

Date	Mileage	Oil Changed	Rotate/ Balance Tires	Air Filters	Tires Replaced	Battery Replaced	Brakes Serviced	Belts & hoses Checked	Wheel alignment	Radiator	Viper Blades	Transmission	Car washed	Cost

Other Maintenance		
Date/ Time	Destination/ Place	Mileage

Date	Mileage	Oil Changed	Rotate/ Balance Tires	Air Filters	Tires Replaced	Battery Replaced	Brakes Serviced	Belts & hoses Checked	Wheel alignment	Radiator	Viper Blades	Transmission	Car washed	Cost

Other Maintenance		
Date/ Time	Destination/ Place	Mileage

Made in the USA
Columbia, SC
20 November 2020